# Building Strong Teams

## *A Comprehensive Guide to Team Building*

***Gerard Assey***

# Building Strong Teams:
## *A Comprehensive Guide to Team Building*

By

Gerard Assey



*Published by:*
Gerard Assey
19/18, Palli Arasan Street
Anna Nagar East
Chennai - 600 102

**ISBN:** 978-81-971121-8-8

# Table of Contents


- ✓ Preface
- ✓ Team Management –Essential for the Success of any Organization
- ✓ Core Skills for Team Management
- ✓ Qualities/Characteristics of High-Performing Teams
- ✓ Building a High-Performing, Strong, Cohesive Team
- ✓ Improving Team Synergy and Creating High-Performing Teams
- ✓ Handling Difficult Team Members
- ✓ Getting Employees Excited About Being in a Team
- ✓ Motivating Teams to Improve Performance
- ✓ Keeping Teams Highly Motivated
- ✓ The Importance of Positive Feedback
- ✓ Team Building Ideas
- ✓ Engaging and Fun-Filled Team Building Activities
- ✓ Addressing Common Workplace Challenges
- ✓ Building and Maintaining High-Performing Teams: A Step-by-Step Guide
- ✓ Team Building Toolkit
- ✓ Conclusion
- ✓ About the Author

# Preface

Welcome to the world of team building! This book is a comprehensive guide designed to help organizations build and maintain strong, cohesive teams that drive success and innovation. Whether you're a seasoned team leader looking to enhance your skills or a newcomer seeking guidance on how to build effective teams, this book has something for you.

In today's fast-paced and competitive business environment, the ability to work effectively as a team is more important than ever. Teams that communicate well, collaborate effectively, and support each other are better equipped to tackle challenges, achieve goals, and drive organizational success.

This book covers a wide range of topics related to team building, including communication, leadership, motivation, and conflict resolution. Each chapter provides practical strategies, actionable tips, and real-world examples that you can apply in your own organization to enhance team performance and drive results.

Throughout the book, you'll find interactive elements such as quizzes, reflection questions, and team-building activities that will help you engage with the material and apply it to your own team-building efforts. Additionally, a comprehensive Team Building Toolkit at the end of the book provides templates, checklists, and guides to help you plan and execute successful team-building activities.

Whether you're a manager looking to improve team dynamics, an HR professional seeking to enhance employee engagement, or a team member eager to contribute more effectively, this book will provide you with the tools and strategies you need to succeed.

Thank you for embarking on this team-building journey with us. We hope that the insights and ideas presented in this book will inspire you to create strong, cohesive teams that achieve remarkable results.

***Happy team building!***

# Team Management –Essential for the Success of any Organization

Team management is the art and science of guiding a group of individuals towards a common goal. It involves understanding each team member's strengths and weaknesses, effectively delegating tasks, fostering open communication, and providing support and guidance as needed. Effective team management is crucial for the success of any organization as it helps in maximizing productivity, improving morale, and achieving better results.

One of the key benefits of effective team management is improved productivity. When team members feel valued and motivated, they are more likely to put in their best effort, leading to increased efficiency and output. Effective team management also fosters innovation and creativity by encouraging collaboration and idea-sharing among team members. When individuals from diverse backgrounds come together to work towards a common goal, they bring unique perspectives and ideas to the table, which can lead to breakthrough innovations and solutions.

Another benefit of effective team management is improved morale and job satisfaction. When team members feel supported and appreciated, they are more likely to be engaged and satisfied with their work. This, in turn, leads to lower turnover rates and higher employee retention, saving the organization time and resources that would otherwise be spent on recruiting and training new employees.

Effective team management also leads to better communication and decision-making. When team members are encouraged to communicate openly and honestly, misunderstandings and conflicts can be resolved quickly, leading to smoother workflow and better outcomes. Additionally, effective team management involves empowering team members to make decisions and take ownership of their work, which can lead to quicker and more informed decision-making.

In conclusion, effective team management is essential for the success of any organization. By understanding the importance of team management and its benefits, organizations can create a positive and productive work environment that fosters innovation, creativity, and success.

# Core Skills for Team Management

Effective team management requires a combination of core skills that enable leaders to guide their teams towards success. These skills include leadership, planning, communication, compassion, consistency, drive, development, and accountability.

- ✓ **Leadership** is perhaps the most critical skill for effective team management. A good leader inspires and motivates team members, sets clear goals, and provides direction. They lead by example, earning the respect and trust of their team.
  Example: A leader in a software development team sets a vision for creating a user-friendly product. They inspire the team by highlighting the impact the product will have on users.
  Action Plan: Attend leadership training programs, seek mentorship from experienced leaders, practice active listening, and lead by example.
- ✓ **Planning** is essential for ensuring that team goals are achieved efficiently. A good leader develops a clear roadmap for how goals will be achieved, including setting deadlines, allocating resources, and identifying potential obstacles.
  Example: A project manager creates a detailed project plan outlining tasks, timelines, and resources required for each phase of the project.
  Action Plan: Use project management tools, break down tasks into smaller, manageable

steps, and regularly review and adjust plans as needed.

- ✓ **Communication** is key to successful team management. A good leader communicates openly and honestly with their team, ensuring that everyone is on the same page. They listen actively to their team members' feedback and ideas, fostering a culture of collaboration and trust.
  Example: A team leader conducts regular team meetings to discuss project progress, challenges, and updates.
  Action Plan: Improve active listening skills, provide clear and concise instructions, encourage open communication, and use various communication channels effectively.
- ✓ **Compassion** is an often overlooked but important skill for effective team management. A good leader shows empathy towards their team members, understanding their needs and concerns. They provide support and encouragement, helping team members overcome challenges and grow professionally.
  Example: A manager shows compassion by understanding and accommodating a team member's personal challenges while still ensuring project deadlines are met.
  Action Plan: Practice empathy, show appreciation for team members' efforts, offer support and assistance, and create a supportive work environment.
- ✓ **Consistency** is crucial for building trust and credibility as a leader. A good leader is consistent in their actions and decisions,

ensuring that team members know what to expect and can rely on them.

Example: A leader consistently applies the organization's policies and procedures, ensuring fairness and equality among team members.

Action Plan: Develop a routine for managing tasks, set clear expectations, and maintain regular communication with team members.

- ✓ **Drive** is what propels a team towards achieving its goals. A good leader is driven to succeed and inspires the same drive in their team members. They set high standards and push their team to exceed them.

  Example: A sales manager motivates their team to achieve sales targets by setting challenging but achievable goals and providing incentives for top performers.

  Action Plan: Set ambitious yet realistic goals, stay focused on objectives, seek feedback for continuous improvement, and maintain a positive attitude.

- ✓ **Development** involves helping team members grow both personally and professionally. A good leader provides opportunities for training and development, helping team members acquire new skills and advance their careers.

  Example: A team leader identifies training opportunities for team members to enhance their skills and advance their careers.

  Action Plan: Encourage continuous learning, provide opportunities for skill development, offer constructive feedback, and recognize and reward growth.

- ✓ **Accountability** is essential for ensuring that team goals are met. A good leader holds themselves and their team members accountable for their actions and performance, ensuring that everyone takes responsibility for their work.
  Example: A project manager holds team members accountable for meeting project deadlines and delivering quality work.
  Action Plan: Set clear expectations and goals, establish regular check-ins to monitor progress, provide constructive feedback, and lead by example by taking responsibility for mistakes.

In conclusion, these core skills are essential for effective team management. By developing these skills, leaders can build strong, high-performing teams that achieve their goals and drive organizational success.

# Qualities/Characteristics of High-Performing Teams

Here's a detailed exploration of each quality or characteristic of high-performing teams, along with examples and action plans for developing them:

**1. Clear Goals and Vision:**

- ✓ Example: A marketing team has a clear goal of increasing brand awareness by 20% in the next quarter. This goal is communicated to all team members, who understand how their individual efforts contribute to this larger objective.
- ✓ Action Plan: Define specific, measurable, achievable, relevant, and time-bound (SMART) goals. Ensure alignment between individual and team goals. Regularly review and communicate progress towards these goals.

**2. Open Communication:**

- ✓ Example: A software development team holds regular stand-up meetings where team members openly discuss their progress, challenges, and ideas. They also have a feedback loop where team members can provide input on each other's work.
- ✓ Action Plan: Encourage a culture of transparency and trust. Establish regular communication channels, such as meetings, emails, or chat platforms. Encourage active listening and provide opportunities for feedback.

3. **Strong Leadership:**
   - ✓ Example: A project manager leads by example, demonstrating strong decision-making skills, effective communication, and a clear vision for the project. They also provide support and guidance to team members.
   - ✓ Action Plan: Develop leadership skills through training and mentorship. Practice empathy and understanding. Lead by example and inspire others to follow your lead.
4. **Trust and Respect:**
   - ✓ Example: A sales team trusts each other to meet their individual targets, knowing that everyone is committed to the team's success. They also respect each other's opinions and ideas, even when they disagree.
   - ✓ Action Plan: Build trust by being reliable and consistent. Respect others' opinions and perspectives. Communicate openly and honestly. Address conflicts promptly and respectfully.
5. **Collaboration:**
   - ✓ Example: A cross-functional team collaborates on a project, bringing together different skills and perspectives to achieve a common goal. They regularly share information, resources, and ideas.
   - ✓ Action Plan: Foster a collaborative environment by encouraging teamwork and cooperation. Break down silos between departments. Provide opportunities for team members to work together on projects.
6. **Adaptability**:
   - ✓ Example: A customer service team quickly adapts to changing customer needs and

market trends. They are open to trying new approaches and technologies to improve their service.

- ✓ Action Plan: Develop a mindset of flexibility and resilience. Encourage experimentation and innovation. Learn from failures and adapt strategies accordingly.

**7. Innovation:**

- ✓ Example: A product development team regularly generates new ideas for product improvements and features. They experiment with new technologies and methodologies to stay ahead of the competition.
- ✓ Action Plan: Encourage creativity and out-of-the-box thinking. Provide resources and support for innovation. Celebrate and reward innovative ideas and successes.

**8. Accountability:**

- ✓ Example: A project team holds each member accountable for their individual tasks and deadlines. They have regular check-ins to review progress and address any issues that may arise.
- ✓ Action Plan: Set clear expectations and responsibilities. Establish a system for tracking progress and holding team members accountable. Provide support and resources to help team members meet their goals.

**9. Recognition and Reward:**

- ✓ Example: A sales team recognizes top performers with bonuses, awards, or public recognition. This motivates other team members to strive for excellence.
- ✓ Action Plan: Establish a system for recognizing and rewarding outstanding

performance. Make recognition timely and specific. Ensure that rewards are meaningful and aligned with team goals.

**10. Continuous Learning and Improvement:**

- ✓ Example: A marketing team regularly attends workshops and training sessions to stay updated on the latest trends and techniques in digital marketing. They also conduct post-project reviews to identify areas for improvement.
- ✓ Action Plan: Encourage a culture of learning and development. Provide opportunities for training and skill-building. Encourage team members to seek feedback and learn from their experiences.

By focusing on developing these qualities and characteristics, teams can enhance their performance, achieve their goals, and drive organizational success.

# Building a High-Performing, Strong, Cohesive Team

Building a high-performing, strong, and cohesive team requires a strategic approach that focuses on hiring the right people, building trust and respect, fostering a positive team culture, encouraging collaboration, and providing opportunities for growth and development. Here's a detailed explanation of each step with examples and action plans:

**1. Hiring the Right People:**

- ✓ Example: A software development company hires candidates not just based on technical skills but also on their fit with the team culture and values. They look for candidates who are team players, adaptable, and share the company's vision.
- ✓ Action Plan: Develop a comprehensive hiring process that includes behavioral interviews, skills assessments, and cultural fit evaluations. Clearly define the qualities and attributes you're looking for in candidates. Involve team members in the hiring process to ensure alignment with team dynamics.

**2. Building Trust and Respect:**

- ✓ Example: A sales team builds trust by openly sharing information, respecting each other's opinions, and supporting each other in achieving common goals. They also address conflicts and disagreements respectfully and constructively.
- ✓ Action Plan: Lead by example by demonstrating trust and respect towards team members. Encourage open communication

and feedback. Establish team norms that promote trust and respect. Address any issues or conflicts promptly and fairly.

**3. Fostering a Positive Team Culture:**

- ✓ Example: A marketing team fosters a positive culture by celebrating successes, acknowledging contributions, and creating a supportive environment where team members feel valued and motivated.
- ✓ Action Plan: Define and communicate the team's values and goals. Encourage teamwork and collaboration. Organize team-building activities and events. Provide regular feedback and recognition for individual and team achievements.

**4. Encouraging Collaboration:**

- ✓ Example: A project management team encourages collaboration by using collaborative tools and technologies, such as project management software and communication platforms. They also hold regular team meetings and brainstorming sessions to foster collaboration.
- ✓ Action Plan: Create a collaborative work environment by providing tools and resources that facilitate communication and collaboration. Encourage open and honest communication. Foster a culture of sharing ideas and knowledge. Assign tasks that require collaboration and teamwork.

**5. Providing Opportunities for Growth and Development:**

- ✓ Example: A human resources team provides opportunities for growth and development through training programs, mentorship, and career development plans. They also encourage employees to pursue further education and certifications.

- ✓ Action Plan: Identify and prioritize areas for growth and development within the team. Provide access to training programs, workshops, and seminars. Offer opportunities for mentorship and coaching. Create career development plans for team members.

By implementing these strategies and focusing on these key areas, organizations can build high-performing, strong, and cohesive teams that are equipped to achieve their goals and drive success.

# Improving Team Synergy and Creating High-Performing Teams

Improving team synergy and creating high-performing teams requires a combination of team building activities, encouraging open communication, setting clear goals and expectations, and providing regular feedback. Here's a detailed explanation of each step with examples and action plans:

**1. Team Building Activities and Exercises:**

- ✓ Example: A marketing team participates in a team-building retreat where they engage in activities such as trust falls, problem-solving challenges, and team bonding exercises. These activities help build trust, improve communication, and foster collaboration.
- ✓ Action Plan: Schedule regular team-building activities, such as workshops, retreats, or outdoor adventures. Choose activities that focus on specific goals, such as improving communication, building trust, or enhancing problem-solving skills. Ensure that activities are inclusive and cater to the interests and abilities of all team members.

**2. Encouraging Open Communication:**

- ✓ Example: A project team holds regular meetings where team members are encouraged to share their thoughts, ideas, and concerns openly. They also use communication tools such as email, chat, and project management software to stay connected and informed.
- ✓ Action Plan: Create a culture of open communication by setting an example as a

leader. Encourage team members to speak up and share their opinions. Use communication tools effectively to facilitate communication. Provide opportunities for feedback and encourage active listening.

3. **Setting Clear Goals and Expectations:**
   - ✓ Example: A sales team sets specific, measurable, achievable, relevant, and time-bound (SMART) goals for each quarter. These goals are communicated to all team members, along with clear expectations for performance and outcomes.
   - ✓ Action Plan: Define clear goals and objectives for the team, ensuring that they are aligned with the overall goals of the organization. Communicate these goals to all team members and ensure that everyone understands their role in achieving them. Provide regular updates on progress towards goals and adjust expectations as needed.
4. **Providing Regular Feedback:**
   - ✓ Example: A customer service team receives regular feedback from customers through surveys and feedback forms. They also receive feedback from their manager through performance reviews and one-on-one meetings.
   - ✓ Action Plan: Establish a system for providing regular feedback to team members. Schedule regular performance reviews and check-ins to discuss progress and areas for improvement. Provide constructive feedback that is specific, actionable, and focused on behavior or outcomes.

By implementing these strategies and focusing on improving team synergy, organizations can create high-performing teams that are more effective, efficient, and motivated to achieve their goals.

# Handling Difficult Team Members

Handling difficult team members requires a thoughtful and proactive approach. Here's a detailed explanation of each step with examples and action plans:

**1. Identifying the Root Cause of Behavior:**

- ✓ Example: A team member consistently misses deadlines and appears disengaged. After a one-on-one discussion, it becomes clear that they are overwhelmed with their workload and feel unsupported.
- ✓ Action Plan: Schedule a private meeting to discuss their behavior. Listen actively to understand their perspective. Offer support and resources to help them manage their workload and address any underlying issues.

**2. Communicating Effectively:**

- ✓ Example: A team member is frequently disruptive during meetings. The team leader addresses this behavior by having a private conversation to explain the impact it has on the team's productivity and morale.
- ✓ Action Plan: Use clear and direct communication to address the behavior. Focus on the specific behavior that needs to change and explain why it is problematic. Encourage open dialogue and listen to their perspective.

**3. Setting Clear Expectations and Consequences:**

- ✓ Example: A team member consistently arrives late to work. The team leader sets a clear expectation that they must be punctual and outlines the consequences, such as a verbal warning or disciplinary action, if the behavior continues.

- ✓ Action Plan: Clearly communicate expectations regarding behavior, performance, and deadlines. Outline the consequences of not meeting these expectations. Follow through consistently with consequences if necessary.

**4. Offering Support and Guidance:**

- ✓ Example: A team member is struggling to meet performance goals. The team leader provides additional training, assigns a mentor, and meets regularly to offer guidance and support.
- ✓ Action Plan: Identify the specific areas where the team member needs support. Provide resources, training, or mentorship to help them improve. Offer regular feedback and encouragement to keep them motivated.

Overall, handling difficult team members requires empathy, clear communication, and a willingness to address issues promptly and effectively. By identifying the root cause of behavior, communicating effectively, setting clear expectations, and offering support and guidance, you can help difficult team members improve their performance and become valuable contributors to the team.

# Getting Employees Excited About Being in a Team

Excitement within a team isn't manufactured through motivational posters or annual retreats. It comes from something deeper—something that speaks to the human desire to belong, to matter, and to grow. Employees become genuinely excited about being in a team when they feel that they are part of something bigger than themselves, when their work is seen and appreciated, and when they believe that their future is being nurtured. This chapter dives into how to create that emotional buy-in by building a strong sense of purpose, celebrating team wins in meaningful ways, and fostering real growth and development. These strategies go beyond theory; they are rooted in real workplace dynamics and can be implemented starting today.

## Creating a Sense of Purpose and Belonging

The foundational step in creating an excited team is to answer the silent question every employee has: "Why does what I do matter?" People need to feel that they are not just filling a role—they are contributing to a mission. The moment they connect their daily tasks to a greater cause, energy and commitment rise organically.

Let's take the example of a logistics team in a large e-commerce company. Their job may seem mundane—packing, shipping, tracking—but when leadership took time to share customer feedback, testimonials, and videos of how timely deliveries helped families celebrate birthdays and milestones, everything changed. What was once viewed as routine became a mission: "We deliver smiles." That simple shift in narrative created ownership, pride, and emotional engagement.

Creating belonging goes hand in hand with purpose. It means fostering a culture where people feel safe, heard, and included. This is where small, consistent actions matter—leaders checking in regularly (not just when something's wrong), team meetings where everyone has a voice, rituals that make people feel seen.

Action Plan: Start by crafting a purpose statement for your team. Involve everyone in this conversation. Ask questions like, "Who do we serve?" "How do we make life better for others?" Then, reinforce this purpose in team huddles, visual boards, or internal newsletters. Create onboarding processes that introduce new hires not just to the workflow, but to the story of the team—where it came from, what it stands for, and where it's going. Host a "Belonging Day" quarterly, where each person shares a personal story about what working in the team means to them. These simple, heartfelt practices embed belonging deeply into the team's DNA.

**Celebrating Successes and Milestones**

Celebration is not an afterthought—it is the fuel that keeps teams moving forward. When teams achieve a goal, overcome a challenge, or hit a milestone, it's critical that those moments are acknowledged with joy and shared meaning.

But celebration doesn't always mean grand gestures or expensive outings. It can be something as simple as decorating the office space after completing a project, creating a highlight reel of team accomplishments, or organizing a surprise lunch. In one customer service team, every time they met their monthly resolution target, the team leader brought in cupcakes with each team member's name on it. The team eventually began calling it "Cupcake Fridays," and it became a cherished tradition. Morale soared—not because of the cupcakes, but because someone took the time to celebrate them in a personal, consistent way.

Celebrating individual milestones is just as important. A work anniversary, the birth of a child, completion of a professional course—these should be embraced as part of the team's collective joy. Recognizing life outside work creates emotional connection inside work.

Action Plan: Set up a calendar of celebrations for the team—project completions, birthdays, tenure anniversaries. Appoint a "Celebrations Champion" from within the team to lead the planning each month. Make each celebration unique and personal. For major achievements, involve senior leaders in the celebrations to show visibility and support. After every celebration, invite team feedback: "How did this make you feel?" "What else can we celebrate next time?" This loop of inclusion ensures celebrations stay relevant and inspiring.

**Providing Opportunities for Growth and Development**

If the team feels like a place where careers go to stagnate, no amount of celebration or purpose will keep motivation high for long. People need to feel they are moving forward—not just in their job titles, but in their skills, their confidence, and their ability to contribute.

Growth and development should be built into the team's structure, not added as an afterthought. This means identifying learning goals for each team member during performance discussions and crafting personalized development plans. A great example comes from a mid-sized IT firm, where the HR department initiated a "Skill Swap Week" every quarter. Each employee could sign up to teach a skill they were good at—be it Excel automation, customer empathy, or presentation design—while attending sessions offered by peers. It cost nothing, but created a culture of learning, mutual respect, and shared expertise.

Growth also includes giving people a chance to lead. Allowing team members to take charge of small projects, lead meetings, or mentor new hires builds confidence and injects excitement into everyday work. When people see that their current role is a stepping stone and not a dead end, they become engaged, hopeful, and loyal.

Action Plan: Begin by having individual development conversations with each team member. Ask what skills they want to develop, what roles they dream of stepping into, and what challenges excite them. Build quarterly development goals and provide resources—online courses, job shadowing, stretch assignments. Create "Growth Check-Ins" every month where team members share what they've learned or achieved. Celebrate development as passionately as you celebrate project delivery.

Getting employees excited about being in a team is not a checkbox to tick—it's an ongoing journey that requires thought, heart, and strategy. It begins with making people feel they are part of something meaningful. It flourishes when achievements are acknowledged joyfully. And it endures when growth is intentional and celebrated.

When team members wake up looking forward to working with each other, when they feel valued and seen, and when they know that their future is in good hands, excitement is no longer something you have to create—it becomes a natural byproduct of great leadership and culture. That's the kind of team everyone wants to be part of. That's the kind of team that changes everything.

# Motivating Teams to Improve Performance

Motivation is the heartbeat of performance. Without it, even the most talented teams can fall short of expectations. But when motivation is nurtured intentionally, with well-thought-out strategies and a genuine understanding of what drives people, it becomes the catalyst for excellence. In this chapter, we will explore how to motivate teams to improve performance by establishing challenging goals, offering meaningful incentives, recognizing achievements, and providing advancement opportunities—each backed by practical action plans and real-world examples.

**Setting Challenging Goals**

People thrive when they feel stretched—not stressed, but challenged. The right goals push teams beyond their comfort zones while still feeling attainable with effort. Goals that are too easy breed complacency; goals that are unrealistic create frustration. The sweet spot is in goals that require growth, collaboration, and focus.

To begin with, leaders must first engage their teams in goal-setting. Instead of dictating objectives from the top, involve team members in the goal creation process. This builds ownership. For instance, a marketing team aiming to increase campaign engagement might begin by analyzing past data together, identifying gaps, and then setting a bold target—like increasing conversion rates by 25% over the next quarter.

Once goals are identified, the key is to break them down into smaller action steps with clear deadlines. This prevents overwhelm and allows the team to measure incremental progress. A team lead might implement bi-weekly review meetings where each team member presents their contributions, roadblocks, and insights. These touchpoints serve as motivational check-ins and help identify areas needing course correction.

Action Plan: Use a collaborative goal-setting session. Give teams access to data, allow them to brainstorm targets, and then agree on stretch goals that are realistic but ambitious. Break goals down into 30-day sprints and hold short progress huddles every week. Always link goals to the larger purpose of the organization so that everyone understands the “why.”

**Providing Incentives and Rewards**

Motivation isn't just about internal drive—it is also influenced by external recognition. Thoughtful incentives go a long way in keeping morale high and performance consistent. But the keyword here is “thoughtful.” A one-size-fits-all reward system often misses the mark.

The first step is to understand what drives your team members individually. For some, it's financial bonuses. For others, it's extra time off, public recognition, professional development opportunities, or even a simple hand-written note of appreciation. A project manager once offered high-performing developers the opportunity to attend a tech conference of their choice as a reward for delivering a complex release two weeks ahead of schedule. The effect? Not only did the team beat their deadline—they also came back from the conference with innovative ideas and renewed passion.

The reward must always be timely and directly tied to the effort. Delayed or generic rewards dilute impact. For example, a sales team exceeding their monthly target should not wait until the next quarter to be rewarded. A small celebratory event, a thank-you email copied to leadership, and a bonus added to that month's payroll can make all the difference.

Action Plan: Begin by surveying team members (informally or anonymously) about what types of rewards motivate them. Match rewards to performance milestones, and vary them to keep interest high. Most importantly, celebrate both individual and team efforts regularly—not just at the year-end appraisal.

**Recognizing and Celebrating Achievements**

Recognition is fuel for the human spirit. It tells people they are seen, that their work matters, and that they're not just another cog in the machine. Sadly, this is where many organizations falter—waiting for grand victories instead of celebrating the many small wins along the way.

Daily or weekly recognition rituals can transform workplace morale. In one operations team, the manager started a practice called "Friday Shout-Outs," where each team member could recognize a colleague for something they did that week. It could be anything from solving a client issue creatively to simply stepping in to help with a workload. These were emailed out to the team every Friday at 3 p.m., creating a wave of positivity before the weekend.

Recognition doesn't always need to be loud. A quiet word from a respected leader, a thank-you card left on someone's desk, or a one-minute highlight in a meeting can have lasting effects. The point is to make it personal and sincere.

Action Plan: Create systems and rituals around recognition. Encourage peer-to-peer recognition as well as top-down. Rotate who delivers the recognition, so it feels inclusive and genuine. Track achievements—big or small—and make recognition part of team culture, not just an HR initiative.

**Offering Opportunities for Advancement**

If team members feel that their career is stagnating, no amount of pizza parties or recognition can compensate. The deepest motivation often stems from growth—knowing that one's contribution leads somewhere valuable.

It starts with clarity. Leaders must have regular career conversations with team members. Not just about promotions, but about aspirations, strengths, and developmental paths. If someone expresses an interest in project management, provide them with opportunities to lead small initiatives. If a customer service rep wants to move into training, let them co-facilitate onboarding sessions for new hires.

One company created a "growth track program," where employees could shadow roles in other departments every quarter. Not only did it give employees exposure and fresh perspective, but it also built cross-functional understanding across the business. As a result, internal mobility increased, and motivation spiked—people knew that growth was possible, and that the company was invested in it.

Action Plan: Schedule one-on-one meetings with every team member at least once every quarter to discuss their aspirations. Create a transparent framework for growth and advancement, complete with skill-building plans, mentoring, and stretch assignments. Promote from within wherever possible, and share success stories of those who have climbed the ladder internally.

Motivating teams to improve performance is not a one-time project—it's an ongoing leadership commitment. It demands intentionality, creativity, and emotional intelligence. When teams are presented with clear and compelling goals, supported with the right incentives, recognized sincerely, and given a path to grow, motivation doesn't need to be manufactured—it becomes a natural, self-sustaining force.

Organizations that build these motivational strategies into their DNA find themselves with teams that are not just productive, but passionate, engaged, and loyal. That's not just good leadership—it's smart business.

# Keeping Teams Highly Motivated

**Creating a Positive Work Environment:**

- ✓ Example: A manager creates a positive work environment by fostering a culture of respect, open communication, and collaboration. They encourage teamwork and provide support and encouragement to team members.
- ✓ Action Plan: Foster a positive work environment by promoting open communication, encouraging collaboration, and recognizing and rewarding achievements. Address any issues or conflicts promptly and fairly.

**Encouraging Autonomy and Ownership:**

- ✓ Example: A team is given the freedom to choose how they complete a project, allowing them to take ownership of their work and feel empowered.
- ✓ Action Plan: Delegate tasks and responsibilities to team members, allowing them to make decisions and take ownership of their work. Provide guidance and support as needed, but trust them to deliver results.

**Providing Regular Feedback and Recognition:**

- ✓ Example: A manager provides regular feedback to team members, acknowledging their contributions and providing constructive criticism to help them improve.
- ✓ Action Plan: Schedule regular one-on-one meetings with team members to provide feedback on their performance. Recognize

and reward individual and team achievements. Make feedback specific, timely, and actionable.

**Offering Opportunities for Learning and Development:**

- ✓ Example: A company offers employees the opportunity to attend workshops, seminars, and training programs to enhance their skills and knowledge.
- ✓ Action Plan: Provide opportunities for learning and development, such as training programs, workshops, and seminars. Encourage employees to pursue certifications and further education. Support and encourage continuous learning and improvement.

By implementing these strategies, organizations can keep their teams highly motivated, engaged, and productive.

# The Importance of Positive Feedback

**Benefits of Positive Feedback:**

- ✓ Positive feedback boosts morale and motivation.
- ✓ It reinforces desired behaviors and performance.
- ✓ It improves communication and strengthens relationships.
- ✓ It enhances employee engagement and job satisfaction.

**How to Give Effective Positive Feedback:**

- ✓ Be specific: Clearly identify the behavior or achievement you're praising.
- ✓ Be timely: Give feedback as soon as possible after the event.
- ✓ Be sincere: Express genuine appreciation and gratitude.
- ✓ Be constructive: Connect the feedback to specific outcomes and suggest ways to continue or improve the behavior.

**Examples of Positive Feedback in Action:**

- ✓ "Sarah, I want to commend you for your excellent presentation. Your thorough research and clear delivery really impressed the team."
- ✓ "John, I appreciate your proactive approach to problem-solving. Your initiative in identifying and resolving issues quickly is invaluable to the team."

- ✓ "Emma, your positive attitude and willingness to help others are truly inspiring. Thank you for being such a great team player."

**Action Plan & Strategies:**

- ✓ Implement a regular feedback system: Schedule regular check-ins or performance reviews to provide ongoing feedback.
- ✓ Use a feedback tool: Consider using a feedback tool or platform to facilitate the feedback process and keep track of feedback given.
- ✓ Train managers and team leaders: Provide training on giving effective feedback to managers and team leaders to ensure they are equipped to deliver feedback that is meaningful and impactful.
- ✓ Encourage peer-to-peer feedback: Foster a culture where team members feel comfortable giving and receiving feedback from their peers, not just from managers.
- ✓ Recognize and reward positive behavior: Acknowledge and reward individuals who consistently demonstrate positive behaviors and performance.

# Team Building Ideas

**Outdoor Activities:**

- ✓ Plan a hiking trip to a nearby trail or park.
- ✓ Organize a camping weekend for the team.
- ✓ Arrange a team picnic at a local park or beach.
- ✓ Participate in a ropes course or adventure challenge.
- ✓ Organize a team-building scavenger hunt in the city or town.

**Problem-Solving Challenges:**

- ✓ Conduct a team-building escape room challenge.
- ✓ Organize a puzzle-solving competition.
- ✓ Host a brainstorming session to tackle a real work-related challenge.
- ✓ Create a team-building game that requires problem-solving skills.
- ✓ Set up a series of team challenges with varying levels of difficulty.

**Team-Building Workshops:**

- ✓ Bring in a facilitator to lead a team-building workshop on communication skills.
- ✓ Organize a workshop on conflict resolution and team dynamics.
- ✓ Host a workshop on leadership development and team collaboration.
- ✓ Conduct a workshop on creativity and innovation in the workplace.
- ✓ Arrange a workshop on stress management and team well-being.

**Volunteer Activities:**

- ✓ Volunteer together at a local charity or community organization.
- ✓ Organize a team volunteer day to clean up a park or beach.
- ✓ Participate in a charity event or fundraiser as a team.
- ✓ Volunteer at a local food bank or shelter.
- ✓ Partner with a nonprofit organization for a service project.

Sports Events:

- ✓ Organize a friendly sports tournament, such as soccer, basketball, or volleyball.
- ✓ Participate in a charity run or walk as a team.
- ✓ Attend a professional sports game together.
- ✓ Arrange a team-building day at a local sports facility, such as a batting cage or golf course.
- ✓ Start a team sports league, such as softball or flag football, and compete against other teams.

# Engaging and Fun-Filled Team Building Activities

**Original Ideas for Team Building Activities:**

**The Marshmallow Challenge:** In this activity, teams are given spaghetti, tape, string, and a marshmallow, and they have to build the tallest freestanding structure possible in a set amount of time.

Organizing: Divide participants into teams of four or five. Provide each team with the materials and set a time limit (e.g., 18 minutes). The team with the tallest structure wins.

Feedback: After the activity, discuss the importance of collaboration, communication, and innovation in problem-solving. Ask teams to reflect on their teamwork and what they could have done differently.

**The Human Knot:** Participants stand in a circle, reach in and grab someone else's hand, then try to untangle the knot without letting go of each other's hands.

Organizing: Have participants stand in a circle and randomly grab someone else's hand. Instruct them to untangle the knot without letting go. Set a time limit (e.g., 10 minutes).

Feedback: Discuss the importance of communication, trust, and cooperation. Ask participants how they felt during the activity and what strategies they used to untangle the knot.

**Importance of Fun in Team Building:**

- ✓ Fun activities help break down barriers and build camaraderie among team members.

- ✓ They create a positive and enjoyable work environment, leading to increased morale and motivation.
- ✓ Fun activities can improve communication, collaboration, and problem-solving skills.
- ✓ They can also help reduce stress and improve overall well-being.

**Planning and Executing Team Building Activities:**
Step 1: Identify Goals: Determine the objectives of the team building activities (e.g., improving communication, building trust, enhancing problem-solving skills).
Step 2: Choose Activities: Select activities that align with the goals and interests of the team.
Step 3: Plan Logistics: Arrange for the necessary materials, space, and time for the activities.
Step 4: Communicate: Inform team members about the activities, including the purpose and schedule.
Step 5: Execute: Facilitate the activities, ensuring that everyone is engaged and participating.
Step 6: Debrief: After the activities, facilitate a discussion to reflect on the experience and its impact on team dynamics.
Step 7: Follow-Up: Implement any insights or lessons learned from the activities into daily work practices.

**More Engaging and Fun-filled Team Building Activities**

1. Scavenger Hunt:
   Organizing: Create a list of items or tasks for teams to find or complete within a designated area or time frame. Provide clues or riddles to guide them.

Feedback: Discuss teamwork, problem-solving, and communication skills. Ask teams to share their favorite moments and challenges faced.

2. Escape Room Challenge:

   Organizing: Book an escape room experience where teams work together to solve puzzles and riddles to "escape" the room within a time limit.

   Feedback: Reflect on the importance of collaboration, critical thinking, and time management. Discuss strategies used and lessons learned.

3. Painting or Art Class:

   Organizing: Arrange for a painting or art class where teams create a piece of art together. This activity encourages creativity and collaboration.

   Feedback: Discuss how creativity can be applied to problem-solving in the workplace. Share thoughts on individual contributions to the team art piece.

4. Cooking or Baking Challenge:

   Organizing: Divide teams into groups and assign them a cooking or baking task. This activity promotes teamwork and creativity.

   Feedback: Reflect on the importance of coordination, communication, and adapting to new situations. Enjoy the food prepared together.

5. Team Olympics:

   Organizing: Organize a series of fun and competitive games such as relay races, tug-of-war, and sack races. This activity fosters teamwork and friendly competition.

Feedback: Discuss the importance of sportsmanship, teamwork, and supporting each other. Share highlights and memorable moments from the games.

6. Movie Making Challenge:
   Organizing: Provide teams with a camera or smartphone and a theme. Teams must create a short film or video based on the theme.
   Feedback: Discuss the creative process, collaboration, and effective communication. Watch and enjoy the films together.
7. Office Trivia:
   Organizing: Create a trivia game based on company history, values, and team members' interests. This activity promotes teamwork and knowledge sharing.
   Feedback: Reflect on the importance of knowledge sharing, teamwork, and celebrating achievements. Discuss the most challenging and fun trivia questions.
8. Team Talent Show:
   Organizing: Allow team members to showcase their talents in a talent show format. This activity encourages creativity and builds camaraderie.
   Feedback: Discuss the courage to perform, appreciation for diverse talents, and the importance of supporting each other's interests.
9. Board Game Tournament:
   Organizing: Organize a board game tournament with a variety of games. This activity promotes friendly competition and teamwork.

Feedback: Reflect on the strategies used in the games, teamwork dynamics, and the importance of adaptability and resilience.

10. Community Service Project:
    Organizing: Plan a community service project such as volunteering at a local charity or organizing a donation drive. This activity promotes teamwork and community engagement.
    Feedback: Discuss the impact of the project on the community, teamwork, and personal growth. Share memorable moments and reflections.
11. Team Building Retreat:
    Organizing: Plan a team building retreat at a scenic location. Include activities such as hiking, campfires, and team-building games.
    Feedback: Reflect on the retreat experience, including challenges faced, lessons learned, and the importance of relaxation and team bonding.
12. Karaoke Night:
    Organizing: Host a karaoke night where team members can showcase their singing talents. This activity promotes fun and laughter.
    Feedback: Discuss the importance of stepping out of comfort zones, supporting each other's talents, and building camaraderie.
13. Office Potluck:
    Organizing: Organize a potluck where team members bring dishes to share. This activity promotes teamwork and collaboration.
    Feedback: Reflect on the variety of dishes, teamwork in organizing the potluck, and the enjoyment of sharing a meal together.

14. Team Building Bingo:
    Organizing: Create a bingo card with team building activities or achievements (e.g., "High Five a Teammate," "Complete a Puzzle Together"). Teams must complete the activities to win.
    Feedback: Discuss the fun and challenges of completing the bingo card. Share memorable moments and lessons learned.
15. Storytelling Circle:
    Organizing: Sit in a circle and have each team member share a memorable or funny story from their life. This activity promotes sharing and listening skills.
    Feedback: Reflect on the stories shared, the importance of listening and empathy, and the connections made through storytelling.
16. Mindfulness Meditation Session:
    Organizing: Arrange for a mindfulness meditation session led by an instructor. This activity promotes relaxation and mental well-being.
    Feedback: Discuss the experience of mindfulness meditation, its benefits for stress reduction, and strategies for incorporating mindfulness into daily life.
17. Team Book Club:
    Organizing: Start a team book club where team members read and discuss books related to personal or professional development.
    Feedback: Reflect on the insights gained from the books, the importance of continuous learning, and the value of sharing perspectives with others.

18. Outdoor Adventure Challenge:
    Organizing: Arrange an outdoor adventure challenge at a local adventure park or nature reserve. Activities can include rope courses, zip-lining, rock climbing, and team-building games.
    Feedback: After the challenge, gather the team to reflect on their experiences. Discuss how each member contributed to the team's success, the importance of trust and communication, and strategies used to overcome obstacles. Encourage team members to share their most memorable moments and lessons learned from the challenge.

# Addressing Common Workplace Challenges

Here's a detailed step-by-step guidance on addressing common workplace challenges such as communication breakdowns, conflicts, and lack of motivation, along with examples:

**1. Communication Breakdowns:**

**Identify the Issue:**

Recognize signs of communication breakdowns, such as misunderstandings, lack of clarity, or inconsistent messaging.

**Example:**

Employees are confused about project deadlines due to conflicting information from different team members.

**Develop Action Plan:**

Implement strategies to improve communication, such as regular team meetings, clear communication channels, and active listening practices.

**Example:**

Schedule weekly project update meetings to ensure all team members are on the same page regarding deadlines and project progress.

**Monitor Progress:**

Regularly assess the effectiveness of the communication strategies and make adjustments as needed.

**Example:**

Conduct surveys or feedback sessions to gather input from team members on the impact of the communication improvement efforts.

**2. Conflicts:**

**Identify the Issue:**

Recognize sources of conflicts, such as differences in opinion, competing goals, or personality clashes.

**Example:**

Two team members have conflicting approaches to a project, leading to tension and inefficiency.

**Develop Action Plan:**

Implement conflict resolution strategies, such as mediation, team-building activities, or setting clear expectations and boundaries.

**Example:**

Schedule a mediation session facilitated by a neutral party to help the two team members resolve their differences and find a compromise.

**Monitor Progress:**

Monitor the resolution process and ensure that both parties are actively working towards a solution.

**Example:**

Follow up with the team members involved to assess their progress and provide additional support if needed.

**3. Lack of Motivation:**

**Identify the Issue:**

Recognize signs of demotivation, such as decreased productivity, absenteeism, or lack of enthusiasm.

**Example:**

Team members are not meeting deadlines and seem disengaged during team meetings.

**Develop Action Plan:**

Implement motivational strategies, such as goal setting, recognition programs, or opportunities for skill development.

**Example:**

Set SMART (Specific, Measurable, Achievable, Relevant, Time-bound) goals for each team member and provide regular feedback and recognition for their achievements.

**Monitor Progress:**

Track the impact of the motivational strategies on team members' performance and morale.

**Example:**

Conduct regular performance reviews to assess the effectiveness of the motivational efforts and make adjustments as needed.

By following these steps and implementing tailored solutions, organizations can effectively address common workplace challenges and create a more positive and productive work environment.

# Building and Maintaining High-Performing Teams: A Step-by-Step Guide

**Step 1: Assess Current Team Dynamics**

- ✓ Action Plan: Conduct a team assessment survey to gather feedback from team members on communication, collaboration, and satisfaction levels. Use tools like anonymous surveys or interviews to encourage honest feedback.
- ✓ Example: After analyzing the survey results, identify areas where the team is performing well and areas that need improvement. For instance, if the survey indicates low satisfaction levels with communication, prioritize strategies to enhance communication channels and practices within the team.

**Step 2: Define Clear Team Goals and Objectives**

- ✓ Action Plan: Hold a team meeting to discuss organizational goals and align them with team objectives. Break down larger goals into smaller, SMART (Specific, Measurable, Achievable, Relevant, Time-bound) objectives to ensure clarity and alignment.
- ✓ Example: If the organizational goal is to increase customer satisfaction by 20% within the next year, break down this goal into smaller objectives such as improving response time to customer queries by 15% within the first six months.

**Step 3: Build Trust and Communication**

- ✓ Action Plan: Implement regular team-building activities to foster trust and camaraderie among team members. Encourage open communication by creating channels for feedback and discussion, such as weekly team meetings or virtual collaboration platforms.
- ✓ Example: Organize a team-building retreat where team members participate in trust-building exercises and engage in open discussions about their goals and aspirations. Encourage team members to share their thoughts and ideas openly, creating a culture of transparency and trust.

**Step 4: Develop Strong Leadership**

- ✓ Action Plan: Provide leadership training and coaching sessions to team leaders to enhance their communication, conflict resolution, and coaching skills. Encourage leadership development through mentorship programs and opportunities for additional responsibilities.
- ✓ Example: Offer workshops on effective leadership techniques, such as active listening, giving constructive feedback, and empowering team members. Assign mentors to new team leaders to provide guidance and support as they navigate their roles.

**Step 5: Promote Collaboration and Teamwork**

- ✓ Action Plan: Create cross-functional project teams to encourage collaboration and knowledge sharing across departments. Use tools like project management software or collaborative platforms to facilitate communication and coordination.

- ✓ Example: Assign a cross-functional team to work on a company-wide initiative, such as improving customer experience. Encourage team members from different departments to share their expertise and collaborate on innovative solutions to achieve the project goals.

**Step 6: Provide Opportunities for Growth and Development**

- ✓ Action Plan: Offer training programs, workshops, and certifications to team members to enhance their skills and knowledge. Support career development through performance reviews, goal setting, and opportunities for advancement.
- ✓ Example: Implement a mentorship program where experienced team members mentor junior staff to help them develop new skills and advance their careers. Provide access to online courses and workshops on topics relevant to their roles and career aspirations.

**Step 7: Implement Feedback Mechanisms**

- ✓ Action Plan: Establish regular feedback sessions where team members can provide input on team processes, communication, and performance. Use anonymous surveys or suggestion boxes to encourage honest feedback.
- ✓ Example: Hold quarterly feedback meetings where team members share their thoughts

and ideas for improving team dynamics and processes. Review the feedback received and prioritize action items to address areas of concern.

**Step 8: Celebrate Successes and Milestones**

- ✓ Action Plan: Recognize and celebrate team achievements, both big and small, to boost morale and motivation. Hold team events or ceremonies to acknowledge milestones and accomplishments.
- ✓ Example: Host a monthly "Recognition Day" where team members nominate their peers for outstanding contributions or achievements. Recognize top performers with awards, certificates, or other forms of acknowledgment during team meetings or events.

**Step 9: Monitor and Adjust**

- ✓ Action Plan: Regularly track team performance metrics and key performance indicators (KPIs) to assess progress towards goals. Hold regular check-in meetings to review progress and discuss any challenges or obstacles.
- ✓ Example: Use project management software to track project milestones, deadlines, and resource allocation. Monitor KPIs such as customer satisfaction scores, employee turnover rates, and productivity metrics to identify areas for improvement and make adjustments as needed.

**Step 10: Continuously Improve**

- ✓ Action Plan: Foster a culture of continuous improvement by encouraging experimentation, innovation, and learning. Provide opportunities for team members to share best practices, lessons learned, and innovative ideas.
- ✓ Example: Implement a "lessons learned" session at the end of each project to reflect on successes and challenges and identify opportunities for improvement. Encourage team members to share their insights and propose innovative solutions to enhance team processes and outcomes.

By following this step-by-step plan with detailed examples and action plans, organizations can effectively build and maintain high-performing teams that drive success and innovation.

# Team Building Toolkit

The team building toolkit is designed to provide practical resources for planning and executing team building activities. It includes templates, checklists, and guides that readers can use to implement the ideas discussed in the book.

**Team Building Activity Planning Template:**
This template includes sections for activity objectives, materials needed, timeline, and participant roles. It helps organizers plan and execute team building activities effectively.

Example:
**Feedback Form Template:**
Use this template to collect feedback from participants after team building activities. It includes questions about the activity's impact, organization, and suggestions for improvement.

Example:
**Checklists:**
Pre-Event Checklist:
This checklist outlines the steps to take before a team building activity, such as securing a venue, preparing materials, and communicating with participants.
Example:
Reserve venue
Prepare materials
Send out invitations
Arrange transportation if necessary
Post-Event Evaluation Checklist:

Use this checklist to evaluate the success of a team building activity. It includes questions about participant engagement, learning outcomes, and areas for improvement.

Example:

- ✓ Did participants actively participate in the activities?
- ✓ Were the objectives of the activity achieved?
- ✓ What could be improved for future activities?

**Guides:**

Guide to Effective Team Communication:

This guide provides tips and strategies for improving team communication, including active listening, clear messaging, and resolving conflicts.

Example:

Practice active listening: Focus on what the speaker is saying without interrupting. Ask clarifying questions to ensure understanding.

Guide to Building Trust within Teams:

This guide offers strategies for building trust among team members, such as setting clear expectations, demonstrating reliability, and fostering open communication.

Example:

Be consistent in your actions and follow through on commitments.

Share information openly and transparently with team members.

The team building toolkit provides a comprehensive set of resources for planning, executing, and evaluating team building activities. It is designed to help readers implement the concepts and ideas discussed in the book and improve team dynamics and performance.

---

**Team Building Toolkit**

The Team Building Toolkit is a collection of templates, checklists, and guides designed to help you plan and execute effective team building activities. These resources are intended to be practical and easy to use, providing you with everything you need to create engaging and impactful team building experiences for your team.

**Templates:**

**Team Building Activity Planning Template:**

Objective:

Materials Needed:

Timeline:

Participant Roles:

Feedback Form Template:

Rate the overall effectiveness of the activity (1-5):

What did you enjoy most about the activity?

How could the activity be improved?

**Checklists:**

**Pre-Event Checklist:**

Reserve venue

Prepare materials

Send out invitations

Arrange transportation if necessary

**Post-Event Evaluation Checklist:**

Did participants actively participate in the activities?

Were the objectives of the activity achieved?

What could be improved for future activities?

**Guides:**

**Guide to Effective Team Communication:**

Practice active listening
Use clear and concise language
Encourage open and honest communication
Guide to Building Trust within Teams:
Set clear expectations
Demonstrate reliability
Foster open communication

The Team Building Toolkit is designed to be a flexible resource that can be adapted to suit your team's specific needs. We hope that these tools will help you create engaging and successful team building activities that will strengthen your team's bond and improve overall performance.

# Conclusion

As we come to the end of this journey through the world of team building, we hope that you have gained valuable insights and practical strategies that will help you build and maintain strong, cohesive teams in your organization. Team building is not just about creating a group of people who work together; it's about creating a culture of collaboration, communication, and trust that enables teams to achieve remarkable results.

Throughout this book, we have explored the importance of effective communication, strong leadership, and a positive team culture in driving team success. We have discussed strategies for overcoming common challenges such as communication breakdowns, conflicts, and lack of motivation, and provided actionable tips and examples that you can apply in your own team-building efforts.

We have also emphasized the importance of continuous learning and improvement in team building. Building a high-performing team is an ongoing process that requires commitment, dedication, and a willingness to adapt to change. By implementing the ideas and strategies presented in this book, you can create a work environment where teams thrive, and individuals are empowered to reach their full potential.

As you continue your journey as a team leader, remember that building a strong team is not just about achieving business goals; it's about creating a supportive and inclusive environment where every team member feels valued and respected. By fostering a culture of teamwork and collaboration, you can create a workplace that attracts top talent, drives innovation, and delivers exceptional results.

Thank you for joining us on this team-building adventure. We wish you the very best in your future team-building endeavors. Here's to building strong, cohesive teams that make a difference!

## About the Author
## 'GERARD ASSEY'

Gerard Assey is a Graduate in Economics, a PGD in Management (HRD) and holds a Doctorate in Leadership. Gerard holds several International Qualifications in Sales, Debt Collection, Training & Teaching, and is a 'Fellow' of the prestigious 'Institute of Sales & Marketing Management'-UK, a Certified NLP Practitioner, a 'Certified Trainer', an 'Accredited Management Teacher-Behavioral Sciences', a 'Certified Competency Facilitator', a 'Certified Management Consultant'- (the International credentials of a professional management consultant, awarded in accordance with global standards of the ICMCI); and a Certification from the University of Michigan in 'Successful Negotiation: Essential Strategies and Skills'

He is also a Member of the 'National Association of Sales Professionals' backed with several years experience in varied industries, both in India and Overseas. He also holds an 'Etiquette Consultant' Certification from the USA (by Sue Fox, Author of Best Seller: 'Business Etiquette for Dummies'. She has trained some of the top celebrities' world over). He was also a recipient of a scholarship for extensive training in Japan on 'Corporate Management for India'.

Gerard Assey is 'Founder & Chief Corporate Trainer' of the Group: '**Citius, Altius, Fortius Unlimited'**- an organization that **celebrated 20 years of Glorious Service** in 2021, focusing on 3 Core Competencies:

**People. Performance. Profit**; in functional areas of Sales & Marketing, HR & Organizational Development, covering Recruitment, Training & Consultancy!

Having managed organizations with large Sales Forces in India & Overseas, his specialization cover extensive areas of Sales Training (All levels - Presentation, Negotiation, Key/ Strategic Accounts Management & Managerial Skills for all sectors), Bid Proposal/ Capture Planning/ Management Trainings, Retail Sales, Customer Service & Customer Retention Programs, Training for Prevention & Collection of Debt, Self & Personal Development Programs (Time Management, Teamwork & Team Building, Business Etiquette & Personal Grooming, Leadership & Managerial Skills, People Management Skills, Train-the-Trainer etc), including preparation of Custom-designed Business Manuals for Internal (HR, Induction, and Sales etc) & External use (Instruction, User Manuals).

Gerard has successfully conducted over 6440 Trainings & Workshops (as of Mar '25) all across India, Middle East, Africa, Europe & S.E. Asia. Besides public programs conducted regularly, both in India & Overseas, he has some of the top names as clients whom he services from Single Owners to large Public & Government undertakings, covering all sectors, for their in-house needs.

His website: www.CollectionSkills.com is the only one in this part of the world to be featured in the 'Collections & Credit Risk Magazine-USA' under 'Who's Who in Training' and ranks TOP, along with other websites listed below on most search engines.

**Gerard is author of 187 books already (April 2025),** all the books being available on all online platforms and outlets as E-books and Paperbacks

**A few of our business related books:**

1. Bite-sized Bits on Commonsense Management
2. Heart to Heart on Life's Principles'
3. How to become a Successful Manager
4. The Sales Professionals' Master Workbook of S.Y.S.T.E.M.S
5. The Professional Business Email Etiquette Handbook & Guide
6. The Professional Business Video-Conferencing Etiquette Handbook & Guide
7. Professional Presentation Skills
8. Exceptional Customer Service
9. Professional Tele-Marketing Skills
10. Professional Debt Collection Skills
11. The G.R.E.A.T. Sales & Service Workbook
12. Sales Training Advantage for Results (*The Ultimate Sales Training Manual to enable you stand out as a S.T.A.R.*)
13. CEO Daily Planner & Organizer
14. The Sales Professionals' Master Daily Planner
15. The Professional Debt Collector's Master Daily Planner
16. My Daily Planner & Organizer
17. MY EMERGENCY INFORMATION RECORD (Family Emergency & Peace of Mind Planner)
18. The Ultimate Therapist & Counselors Planner and Organizer
19. Building an Ethical Workplace
20. Managing Relationships at Work
21. Managing Business Meetings Effectively
22. Effective Delegation Skills
23. Goal Setting for Success
24. B2B Selling by Email
25. Professional Business Etiquette & Grooming
26. Dining Etiquette & Table Manners
27. Effective Networking Skills
28. Grooming, Etiquette & Manners for Teens, Young Adults & Future Leaders
29. Inter-Personal Skills
30. Get Ready, Get Hired!
31. Selling in a Recession

32. Effective Receivables Management in an Economic Downturn!
33. Real Estate & Property Sales Training
34. Credit Sales & Accounts Receivable Management
35. Selling Skills for Real Estate & Property Advisors
36. Take G.R.E.A.T. C.A.R.E!
37. Spa, Salon & Health Club Selling Skills
38. Selling Travel, Holiday & MICE Services
39. Selling Skills for Spa's, Salons & Health Clubs
40. Retailing in Salons & Spas
41. Selling Holiday, Vacation, Tours & Packages
42. The Power of Sales Referrals
43. Selling Luxury
44. Technical Selling Skills
45. Financial Advisors Sales Training
46. Dealing with Burnout at Work Monopolize Your Markets
47. Selling to Affluent Customers
48. Growing up with Grace
49. Financial Selling Skills
50. *The Effective Manager's Guide: Key Skills to Thrive*
51. From Aspiring to Inspiring: A Guide for New Managers on the Rise
52. The Power of Focus
53. Selling with Integrity: Sell Like Jesus The Perfect Role Model!
54. 31 Habits of Champions: Your 31-Day Journey to Greatness
55. Rejecting Grasshopper Talk: From Grasshopper to Giant-Killer-*Defeating Giants Daily!*
56. Navigate the AI-Powered Future of Bid & Proposals: Up-Skill to Stay Relevant with Alternative Career Paths & Opportunities
57. Hiring Sales Winners
58. Present with Impact
59. Success Unlocked: *Breaking Free from Habits that Hold You Back*
60. Complaints to Cheers, Feedback to Gold: Mastering Complaints Management
61. Thriving Together: *Cultivating Diversity, Equity, and Inclusion*
62. Coaching Skills for Sales Managers

63. Soaring to Success in Business & Leadership: Swifter, Higher, Stronger!
64. From Classroom to Podium: A Student's Guide to Powerful Public Speaking & Presentation Skills
65. Developing Self-Discipline
66. The CEO's 31-Day Power Plan: Unlocking Success through Essential Traits
67. Credibility Matters
68. A Winning Attitude
69. Bid & Proposal Management Using AI
70. Sales Forecasting: A Practical & Proven Guide to Strategic Sales Forecasting
71. Elevate & Energize: *50 Dynamic & Fun Activities for Peak Workplace Morale*
72. 'Sales SOS! Sales on Fire! *30 Days to Conquer Chaos & the Nightmares of Success!'*
73. Mastering Sales Managerial Skills: *Building High-Performing Teams & Driving Exceptional Results*
74. Eagle-Eyed Leadership: Unleashing the Power of 31 Lessons from Eagles
75. The Ultimate Employee Training Guide: *Training Today, Leading Tomorrow*
76. Being More Accountable at Work
77. Creating a Culture of Continuous Improvement
78. Effective Questioning & Listening Skills
79. The Power of Value Selling
80. The Growth Mindset
81. Mastering Professional Help Desk Skills
82. The Power to Lead with Empathy
83. Being Prepared: The Key to Unlocking Success
84. Youthful Spark-Youth Energizers, Activities and Games-Igniting the Fun in Youth
85. Ignite your Motivation for Success
86. Elevate Your Executive Presence: *Your Roadmap to Executive Excellence*
87. Smart Decisions: *Mastering Problem Solving with Strategic Solutions for Business Success*
88. Strategic Planning: *Developing and Implementing Strategic Plans to Achieve Long-Term Business Goals*
89. The Power of Stay Interviews
90. Developing G.R.I.T.
91. Adaptability

92. Diagnosis- *A Key Skill for Leadership*
93. The Burnout-Proof Salesperson: *The Master Guide to Preventing Stress & Burnout*- Strategies for Thriving in Sales
94. Learning from Failure: *Keys to Success*
95. Customer Success Management
96. Overcoming the Killers of Motivation
97. The C-Suite Code: *Mastering Skills for Executive Excellence'*
98. Dealing with Difficult Customers
99. Unlocking Your Potential: Mastering the Top 20 Life Skills for a Brighter Future
100. Nurturing Tomorrow's Leaders: *Essential Soft Skills Every Child Must Learn*
101. Lively & Fun Party Games for Seniors & Elders
102. Role Playing for Sales Champions: From Practice to Performance
103. Fun and Exciting Party Games for Kids
104. Case Studies for Sales
105. Role-Playing for Unbeatable Customer Service
106. Case Studies in Customer Service
107. Case Studies in Winning Negotiations
108. Case Studies in Management & Leadership
109. Case Studies in Human Resources & Talent Management
110. CEO Success Blueprint: The Essential Toolkit for CEOs and C-Level Executives
111. The Salesperson's Self-Coaching Guide: *Master Your Own Self-Coaching Plan for Success*
112. Overcoming Procrastination: *Your Ultimate Guide to Stop Delaying and Start Living Your Best Life*
113. When True Colors Are Exposed: *The Journey to Unmasking Humanity*
114. Life-Changing Habits for Teens: Teen Success Blueprint for a Bright Future
115. Workplace Stress-Free: *Proven Strategies to Thrive at Work and Beyond*
116. Objection Overruled: *The Ultimate Guide to Turning 'No' into 'Yes'"*
117. Building Strong Teams: *A Comprehensive Guide to Team Building*

Besides regularly contributing to business & trade journals, including international ones such as the 'Creative Training Techniques' and the 'Sales News' of the U.S.A, He is also a member of several prestigious bodies & trade associations, having participated in many Conferences & Workshops in India & Overseas.

Prior to his last assignment of leading & managing a large MNC as head, Gerard had a 3-year stint in the Middle East as a Consultant with a leading British Consultancy Firm.

As the past 'Official Country Representative' for the International Business Award- 'THE STEVIES'-(the business world's own Oscar) for about 4 years- he ensured a few Indian companies that qualify for the same every year!

Gerard can be contacted at:
Email: training@Sales-Training.in,training@CollectionSkills.com
Websites:

www.Sales-Training.in
www.EtiquetteWorks.in
www.CollectionSkills.com
www.RetailSalesTraining.in
www.SalesTrainingIndia.com
www.ManualPreparation.com
www.TrainingWithPuppets.com
www.FirstContactAcademy.com
www.SalesAndMarketingRecruiter.com

## Our TRAININGS that can help your team

- ✓ **Sales Effectiveness**: Selling Skills for any Sector: Service/ Logistics/ FMCG Realty/ Insurance & Finance/ Media/ SPA's, Health Clubs & Salons/ Key Account Management, Effective Negotiation Skills/ Bid & Proposal Management Skills/ Retail Sales Training: Any Sector (Auto, Jewelry, Clothing, Luxury etc)
- ✓ **Customer Service Skills**-Complaints Handling & Customer Retention
- ✓ **Debt Prevention & Collection Skills**
- ✓ **Etiquette & Grooming**
- ✓ **Leadership & Managerial Skills**
- ✓ **Self & Personal Development Skills**: Presentation Skills/ Effective Communication Skills/Business Proposal Writing Skills/ Problem Solving & Decision Making Skills/ Empowering Secretaries-The perfect PA! (For Secretaries & PA's)/ Effective Time Management/ Teamwork & Teambuilding/ P.R.I.D.E- **P**ersonal **R**esponsibility **I**n **D**elivering **E**xcellence

www.ingramcontent.com/pod-product-compliance
Ingram Content Group UK Ltd.
Pitfield, Milton Keynes, MK11 3LW, UK
UKHW021342190726
13845UKWH00027B/673

9 788197 112188